M000290001

CHURCH LIFE IN A CORONAVIRUS WORLD

Contextualizing the Church Today through Lessons from Past Plagues, Famines, and Periods of Persecution

Rev. Michael Peter Sorial

AGORA
UNIVERSITY
PRESS

CHURCH LIFE IN A CORONAVIRUS WORLD

Copyright © 2020 by Agora University Press

All rights reserved. Printed in the United States of America. No part of this book may be used or reproduced in any manner whatsoever without written permission except in the case of brief quotations embodied in critical articles or reviews.

For information contact: aupress@aui.ac

Agora University Press

http://www.aui.ac

ISBN : 978-1-950831-00-5

First Edition (Revised) : July 2020

HIS HOLINESS POPE TAWADROS II

118th Pope and Patriarch of the great city of Alexandria and the See of St. Mark

HIS HOLINESS PATRIARCH IGNATIUS APHREM II

Patriarch of Antioch and All the East

CONTENTS

Acknowledgment

I am using this opportunity to express my deepest gratitude for each person who supported me through this research and writing process. This research project was initially motivated as a means to provide a historical and theological framework for the Coptic Orthodox Archdiocese of North America and the Coptic Diocese of New York and New England during our COVID-19 Task Force planning meetings. At the request of His Grace Bishop David of the Coptic Orthodox Diocese of New York and New England and the priests of the Archdiocese and the Diocese, I was asked to present the findings of the research in a publishable manner. I am grateful for the encouragement they each provided and for the opportunity I was given to engage in such conversations.

As the research was conducted in such a short period of time, it required access provided through a specialized pool of resources and researchers. I am especially thankful to Rafik Adel, a liturgical historian, for his pioneering work and willingness to share without hesitation out of his love for God and his desire to contribute to the development of the Church through this current crisis. I also express my gratitude to Sherif Ramzy, a Coptic researcher, for his continued work in the field.

I would like to also thank Dr. Emmanuel Gergis and Mora Sorial, who provided me with invaluable insights and feedback throughout the research and writing process.

I'm especially grateful to His Holiness Pope Tawadros II for his fatherhood and care for his spiritual children, especially as evidenced by an article he wrote during the coronavirus pandemic titled "The Motherhood of the Church." (See the Appendix for the complete article).

Introduction

If we search through history for times of crisis, it will not take long before we realize that the world seems to have always been in a state of continuous chaos and calamity. Such is the lot of humanity, since the crushing debacle in the garden of Eden. Not until the saving work of our Lord Jesus Christ did humans have hope in the face of the ravenous enemies of death, disease and other devastating forces. In response to, and through union with Christ, Orthodox Christians always sought to remain faithful to shining the light of Jesus in the world within the context of their time and circumstances. History has shown that Christian witness is most spiritually impactful on the world when it emanates from a place of authentic encounter with God.

Just as in times past, with the current coronavirus disease-2019 (hereafter "COVID-19") pandemic, Christians face a fierce dilemma that requires them to address a variety of factors on how to best contextualize the Church in this new Coronavirus World. Ancient faith communities, such as Orthodox Christians, are confronted by numerous issues related to the current pandemic. They must move beyond the rhetoric of 'this is how we have always done things,' especially if they maintain a desire to serve their faithful in a way that does no harm to their unchanging faith.[1]

Throughout my research, I found a consistent stream of evidence emphasizing that during times when liturgical, funerary and other sacramental services required modification, Orthodox Christian communities never lost sight of that which characterized their vocation as disciples of Jesus. As the Church in each generation maintained a focus on the salvation of all of humanity, she[2] never reduced her identity to certain practices or rites. Orthodox Christians always sought to remain aware of the guidance of the Holy Spirit, who was continually directing them to reflect the image of God to the world. History shows that Christ-centered faith communities always flourished after times of great tragedy; whether it was following periods of plague, famine, or persecution, the Church thrived and expanded. This growth was not a result of some imperialistic or worldly ambition, but was rather an unintended result of the Christian response to the theological and spiritual, as well as liturgical and social concerns of the day. After all, if God is the God of the living,[3] then the Church understandably saw herself as the living Body of Jesus Christ, seeking means to actively engage the world around her.

---

[1] Distinction must be made between the essence of faith and its representation in the various forms of practice. For example, the unchanging faith of the Church is that the bread and wine are changed into the true Body and Blood of Christ. This is the essence of the faith. The form of distributing communion has changed its shape over the centuries to include practices like dipping the Body in the Blood, putting the Body in the hands of the faithful, etc. This form can change without impacting the faith of the Church.

[2] It has been customary throughout Christian literature to refer to the *Church* using feminine pronouns (she or her), especially with an emphasis of the imagery of union between Christ the Bridegroom and His bride (the Church).

[3] Mark 12:27.

Today, the Church finds herself in the midst of a global crisis with the Coronavirus pandemic impacting every facet of human life, including various ecclesial practices. It is for that reason that I began exploring historical precedents that may shed light for our current situation. Being a member of an academic community[4] that seeks to address challenges of the contemporary world, it is my desire to produce a work that will respond to many of the questions surrounding the meeting place of an Orthodox faith in the face of crisis. As a priest in the Coptic Orthodox Church, I feel compelled to offer research that will speak to the sensibilities of Orthodox Christians and that is intended to benefit Christians from various traditions. That said, whenever utilizing examples from an Orthodox paradigm (or more specifically from a Coptic experience), I will clarify terms and concepts for the reader.

This research will enable us to assess and offer recommendations for Orthodox Christians during the present times of crisis by answering the question: *How do the lessons from past plagues, famines, and periods of persecution impact the Orthodox Church's response to theological and spiritual questions, liturgical considerations, and social necessities in a Coronavirus world?* I will offer an analysis of the current state of crisis by first investigating the epidemiological and ecclesiological perspectives of the situation, before addressing a variety of issues as they relate to the Eucharist. Next, I will provide a historical analysis of how the Church responded during past plagues, famines, and periods of persecution and consider how some of the lessons may serve the Church in her current time of crisis. Finally, I will discuss some recommendations for how the Church might respond to the current pandemic based on a proper theological paradigm and spiritual trajectory. I believe this

---

[4] I am President and a faculty member at Agora University where I teach a course on "Faith, Culture, and Tradition." For more information, please visit http://www.aui.ac.

study will help provide the Church with the historical precedence to model herself within a 'tradition of diversity' equipped for the challenges of Church life in a Coronavirus world.

Chapter One

COVID-19 Crisis

Times of crisis have the remarkable ability to unearth hidden and unseen symptoms within the human soul. Furthermore, I believe the current Coronavrius pandemic has revealed certain communal opinions within the Church that went long unchecked. Although as humans we tend to compartmentalize matters of science and faith from one another, I will begin by providing a framework for the current crisis, both epidemiologically and ecclesially. Next, I will discuss a variety of questions that have been asked as a result of our current circumstances. Accordingly, I will provide an overview of some of the 'popular'[5] theological understandings of the Eucharist that exist among many of the faithful. Lastly, I will explore whether or not this present *status quo* view of the Eucharist has always been the case.

---

[5] I distinguish the 'popular' theological understanding from the 'ecclesial' theological understanding as there may be a variety of 'popular' myths or folkloric tales that exist among the faithful.

CHURCH LIFE IN A CORONAVIRUS WORLD

Whereas this is primarily a theological and spiritual work – intended to benefit the faithful of the Church – I would be remiss not to address the current crisis from a more holistic view. Although not trained as an epidemiologist, I believe my training as a molecular biologist has afforded me some benefit in analyzing data related to the pandemic. In this first section, I will provide a brief analysis of the current crisis from an epidemiological and ecclesial perspective.

Epidemiological Perspective

On December 31, 2019, the World Health Organization (WHO) was informed of a cluster of pneumonia cases of unknown origin detected in Wuhan City, Hubei Province, China. Within two weeks, the WHO announced that a novel coronavirus had been identified following an initial analysis of virus genetic sequencing from samples taken from some of the earliest infected cases in Wuhan.[6] The virus was referred to as SARS-CoV-2 – popularly known as Coronavirus – and the associated disease as COVID-19.[7] In approximately 100 days following the initial announcement by WHO, as of April 24, 2020, more than 2.66 million cases had been diagnosed globally, with over 190,000 fatalities.[8] A highly infectious respiratory disease, which rapidly spread from person-to-person, the COVID-19 pandemic posed a serious public health risk which seemed to transform the way of life for the entire world in a matter of weeks. Governments, public health partners, corporations, and faith

---

[6] "The Epidemiological Characteristics of an Outbreak of 2019 Novel Coronavirus Diseases (COVID-19)," *China CDC Weekly* 2, no. 8 (2020): 113–22.

[7] In COVID-19, 'CO' stands for 'corona,' 'VI' for 'virus,' 'D' for disease and 19 signifies that this strain of coronavirus first emerged in 2019.

[8] "Situation Update Worldwide, as of 24 April 2020," Epidemiological Updates, *European Centre for Disease Prevention and Control*, April 24, 2020, https://www.ecdc.europa.eu/en/geographical-distribution-2019-ncov-cases.

communities began working closely to respond to the situation. With the ability to cause mild to severe illness, COVID-19 was found to cause the most severe illness in adults 65 years and older and people of any age with serious underlying medical problems. Symptoms ranged from fever, fatigue, dry cough, shortness of breath or difficulty breathing – for individuals displaying mild symptoms – to trouble breathing, persistent pain or pressure in the chest, confusion, or bluish lips or face – for individuals with more severe symptoms.

Some of the distinguishing characteristics of this disease include relatively high morbidity rates, absence of known treatments, tremendous pressure upon the health care system, and fear of dealing with an unknown disease. Therefore, numerous governmental restrictions and recommendations have been issued to mitigate the aggressive spread of COVID-19. Some of these regulations have come in the form of stay-at-home orders, church closures (amongst other businesses deemed 'non-essential'), and mandatory social distancing of at least six feet between persons not from the same household. In the following section, I will discuss the 'crisis of faith' that emerged for many people, based on the aforementioned restrictions and recommendations, specifically as it relates to Church life.

Ecclesial Perspective

By the beginning of March 2020, most Churches had begun discussing – what was deemed by them – responsible action that should be taken in response to the current pandemic. Included in those discussions were matters related to how *regularly scheduled services* would be impacted, what the response of the Church communities would be, and what would be the role of faith in dealing with the disease. One of the points that was at the center of discussion for Orthodox Christians – and Catholic communities, as well as for a few Protestant churches – had to do with the Eucharist. Across social media, in family gatherings, and at Church services, a global debate was raging: 'Would God protect Christians who were taking communion from getting infected?', 'Should the Church consider modifying communion practices?', 'What are the ethical, legal, and medical responsibilities that Christian communities have while navigating through this pandemic?' During all of this, it appeared that there was an absence of discussion around the theological and historical precedence from Church history, which I will address later in this work. Within a matter of weeks, most Churches had implemented some level of social distancing, modified communion practices, or had shifted services to be viewed online.

On Saturday, March 14, 2020, the Coptic Orthodox Archdiocese of North America[9] ('the Archdiocese') and the Coptic Diocese of New York and New England ('Diocese of NYNE') issued a joint statement related to precautions that were being urged by Church leadership to the faithful:

> All non-liturgical services have been immediately suspended in all of our churches until further notice... the faithful are encouraged to use caution when attending Liturgy and are urged to use prudence through appropriate social distancing. For example, when greeting one another, you are asked to greet without touching (as during Pascha Week).[10] If the elderly will attend liturgy during this time, they are encouraged to do so during weekdays, when attendance is

---

[9] The parish I serve at in New Jersey is under the auspices of His Holiness Pope Tawadros II within the jurisdiction of the Coptic Orthodox Archdiocese of North America, placed under the care of His Grace Bishop David (Diocese of New York and New England) who served as the *acting Patriarchal Exarch* on behalf of Pope Tawadros II at the time of the COVID-19 pandemic.

[10] Pascha week for Orthodox Churches is what is popularly referred to as 'Holy Week' for Christians in the West.

expected to be lighter. The faithful are requested to bring their own personal head coverings,[11] personal corporals,[12] and water bottles.[13]

This was a clear step taken by the Coptic Orthodox Church to help mitigate the spread of the disease, even prior to such mandatory governmental decisions in their respective jurisdictions. The following day at Saint Anianus Coptic Orthodox Church, the parish where I serve, Sunday Liturgy was moved to *'the Ark'* – an indoor horse riding arena on the Church property with no heating system – in order to accommodate for social distancing.

Within 48 hours of the initial directive, a second joint statement was issued by the Archdiocese and the Diocese of NYNE on Monday, March 16, 2020. Acknowledging the rapidly evolving situation of the pandemic, the statement was intended to inform the faithful that the Church would "comply with the guidelines of the Centers for Disease Control (CDC) and other public health authorities to limit gatherings to very small numbers. [14] The statement continued to lay out liturgical restrictions, and reiterated a similar sentiment from the first statement, which affirmed the life-giving and healing qualities of the Eucharist. As the first jurisdictions within the Coptic Orthodox Church to take such an action, the

---

[11] A biblical practice taken from 1 Corinthians 11.

[12] Corporals are utilized by the communicants after they have received the Holy Body. In the current practice in the Coptic Orthodox Church, the faithful cover their mouths with a corporal that is usually kept at each respective church and is shared week-to-week.

[13] "COVID-19 Joint Statement" (Coptic Orthodox Archdiocese of North America and Coptic Orthodox Diocese of New York & New England, March 14, 2020). The joint statement may be read in its entirety in the Appendix. The reason the elderly were encouraged to remain at home was due to the understanding that they were at higher risk for the virus.

[14] "2nd Joint Statement Concerning Coronavirus Disease (COVID-19)" (Coptic Orthodox Archdiocese of North America and Coptic Orthodox Diocese of New York & New England, March 16, 2020). The joint statement may be read in its entirety in the Appendix below.

Archdiocese and the diocese of NYNE elicited a reaction from the 'faithful' across social media that spanned the spectrum from anger and accusations of faithlessness to gratitude and encouragement in the face of such opposition.

The Eucharist

As many of the faithful became fearful, a plethora of questions began to pour in. For example, 'How long will this go on for?', 'Is this the end of the world?', 'Is God pouring out His wrath on us?', 'When will we be able to take communion again?' With no end in sight, and Pascha Week around the corner, Coptic Orthodox Churches around the world – along with all other churches – had become relegated to providing 'virtual' services through a combination of YouTube, Zoom, and Facebook Live. For some Christian traditions – especially those not committed to a sacramental pattern of worship – such necessity to move services on-line was in the worst case an inconvenience. However, for Orthodox Christians who maintain the Eucharist as the central act and apex of Christian worship, certain critical questions were brought to the forefront of the discussion. This is a foundational starting point as the Orthodox Christian understanding of Eucharist has always shaped the life and practices of the Church.[15]

Eucharistic Questions Arising from the COVID-19 Crisis

As previously stated, moments of crisis often have a way of forcing people to face certain issues they have taken for granted as a normal part of their way of life. Recent to the onset of COVID-19, I

---

[15] The parallel and connection between Eucharist and the life of the Church finds its genesis in the relationship between Christology and Ecclesiology. Although this is beyond the scope of this work, it is an important connection to make for the sake of the reader.

repeatedly heard countless people stating a variation of the following statement: 'we cannot do things differently because this is the way it has *always* been.' For others, they referred to communion distribution practices as 'the traditional way our church has always done it.' As Orthodox Christians, a faith community that is steeped in 'not changing,' we must be willing to face the difficult questions around areas we may deem to be non-negotiables or that make us uncomfortable. The following are a list of questions that have been discussed in various ecclesial circles and worth further research:

- Is it acceptable for a member of the clergy to hold a private Liturgy?
- What constitutes a private Liturgy?
- If one does not commune for a specified period of time, what risks are involved, if any?[16]
- Should the Church continue to stream Liturgical services? If so, which segments are acceptable to stream?
- Has the Church always distributed communion in the current methodology? If not, how has it been done in the past?
- If the Church were to temporarily modify Eucharistic distribution, what form(s) should she consider?
- How should we respond to people who are 'simple' in faith and would be harmed if the Church made – what they consider to be significant – changes?

---

[16] This again arises from a folkloric tale that lack of communion for a prolonged period of time might result in being possessed by an evil spirit. The tradition of the Church provides multiple examples of many saints, monastics, ascetics and anchorites who lived in the desert for decades without access to the Eucharist like St. Anthony and St. Mary of Egypt. Additionally, in other traditions like the Ethiopian Orthodox Church, the faithful rarely commune during a calendar year.

Although several of these questions reveal a folkloric view of the Eucharist, I believe this time of unearthing erroneous ideas is beneficial to the faithful in moving towards a more accurate theological paradigm and will henceforth have the benefit of correcting their spiritual trajectory. Although I will not attempt to address all of the above questions, I believe it is essential to parse through this issue, as the Orthodox Christian understanding of Eucharist shapes all that is done both within the Divine Liturgy, as well as in the liturgy after the Liturgy.[17]

Was this Always the Case?

Since the Eucharist is directly tied to our understanding of the Incarnation,[18] it is critical that we consider our Eucharistic practice in light of the entire Church. Orthodox practice of the Eucharist is directly tied to Christology[19] and Ecclesiology[20] which both point to what we believe about Christ. This belief must be revealed through the life of the Church in the world. St. Irenaeus of Lyons, a late 2nd century Bishop, stated that "our way of thinking is attuned to the Eucharist, and the Eucharist in turn confirms our way

---

[17] In utilizing the phrase 'liturgy after the Liturgy', I intend to highlight the continued work of the people that they are to engage in following their time of worship in the Divine Liturgy. The liturgy after the Liturgy is thus a natural continuation and culmination of the realization and manifestation of the Body of Christ in the World.

[18] The Orthodox doctrine of the Incarnation is that Jesus Christ, the eternal Word of God, is truly God and truly Human; following the incarnation His humanity parted not from His divinity for a single moment.

[19] Christology is understood as the Church's theological understanding relating to the person, nature, and role of Jesus Christ.

[20] Ecclesiology is understood as the Church's theological understanding relating to the identity, nature, and role of the Church, in particular in her relationship to Christ.

of thinking."[21]

Unfortunately, as discussed earlier, today many believers have reduced the Eucharist simply to some magical potion that they take in order to protect themselves from devils. This understanding is based on a folkloric belief that if they do not commune at least every forty days, a devil will possess them. Others erroneously believe that if they attend Liturgy and take communion, something will automatically transform within them in a more mechanical way. Still others have come to believe that if they take communion before the start of a school year, taking an exam, or having a job interview, this will assure them success in the initiatives they are pursuing.

Although I am not a Eucharistic Theologian, a cursory reading of various Church fathers shows a far different emphasis and focus on the importance of the Eucharist. It can be unequivocally seen in the Bible and patristic writings that the Eucharist is indeed the central act of worship for the Church. Why was the emphasis of the Church on the Eucharist? Early Christians understood the Eucharistic meal in light of the life-giving gift of salvation offered to them by God, as both a means and a sign for a union with God – and between Christians – that is far more intimate than most people have ever considered possible. In his letter to the Church in Philadelphia, St. Ignatius of Antioch highlights the essential quality of unity with the Lord and with each other as he says:

> Take heed, then, to have but one Eucharist. For there is one flesh of our Lord Jesus Christ, and one cup to [show forth] the unity of His blood; one altar; as there is one bishop, along with the presbytery and deacons, my fellow-servants: that so, whatsoever you do, you may do it

---

[21] Irenaeus of Lyons, *Against the Heresies*, vol. 4, 180, 18,5:PG 7/1,1028.

CHURCH LIFE IN A CORONAVIRUS WORLD
according to [the will of] God.[22]

Whether it is in Pauline theology or in early patristic writing, the central act of worship in the Eucharist was declarative and reflective of a shared life that went far beyond what could be perceived by the human eye. The writer of the *Didache*[23] drew a connection between the Eucharistic bread and the Church stating: "even as this broken bread was scattered over the hills, and was gathered together and became one, so let Your Church be gathered together from the ends of the earth into Your kingdom; for Yours is the glory and the power through Jesus Christ forever."[24] The Eucharist therefore was not just something that the Christians did – whether as an act of submitting in obedience to Christ, memorializing past events, receiving some benefits from God, or just gathering socially – but rather it was to come together to reflect, in reality, the Body of Christ.

For anyone who has attended an Orthodox Eucharistic Liturgy, it is clear that there is something unquestionably other-worldly that is happening. Not only is Christ offering Himself to the Church, but she – in reality – is becoming the Body of Christ through union with His Holy Body offered in the Eucharist. St. Augustine expounds on this as he states:

> [The] wholly redeemed city, the assembly and society of the saints, is offered to God as a universal sacrifice by the high priest who in the form of a slave went so far as to offer himself for us in his Passion, to make us the Body of so great a head...Such is the sacrifice of Christians: "we who are many are one Body in Christ." The Church

---

[22] Ignatius of Antioch, *Epistle to Philadelphia*, 4.

[23] The *Didache* (Greek for 'The Teaching'), is a brief late first century treatise that is included in the writings of the Apostolic fathers.

[24] Ibid, 9.

continues to reproduce this sacrifice in the sacrament of the altar so well-known to believers wherein it is evident to them that in what she offers she herself is offered.[25]

Although St. Augustine highlights the process of becoming one body in Christ – perhaps emphasizing the communal aspects of the Eucharist – St. Gregory of Nyssa affirms the personal act of 'becoming' through union with the Immortal One:

> This Body, by the indwelling of God the Word, has been made over to divine dignity. Rightly then, do we believe that the bread consecrated by the word of God has been made over into the Body of God the Word. For that Body was, as to its potency, bread; but it has been consecrated by the lodging there of the Word, who pitched His tent in the flesh. From the same cause, therefore, by which the bread that was made over into that Body is made to change into divine strength, a similar result now takes place. As in the former case, in which the grace of the Word made holy that body the substance of which is from bread, and in a certain manner is itself bread, so in this case too, the bread, as the Apostle says, "is consecrated by God's word and by prayer"; not through its being eaten does it advance to become the Body of the Word, but it is made over immediately into the Body by means of the word, just as was stated by the Word, "This is My Body!"...In the plan of His grace He spreads Himself to every believer by means of that Flesh, the substance of which is from wine and bread, blending Himself with the bodies of believers, so that by this union with the Immortal, man, too, may become a participant in incorruption. These things He bestows through the power of the blessing which transforms the nature of the visible things to that [of the Immortal].[26]

There is a clear unity in the early Christian belief that the Eucharist is the life-giving Body and precious Blood of our Lord, which was given for the sake of salvation, forgiveness of sins, and

---

[25] Augustine of Hippo, *City of God*, 10,6:PL 41,283.

[26] Gregory of Nyssa, *The Great Catechism*, 37.

eternal life for all who partake. However, there appears to be a great deal of diversity in how distribution occurred during different time periods. In other words, the undertone of patristic writings on the Eucharist is very much focused on the 'what' and the 'why', more so than it is on the 'how'. Differences in communion practices can be categorized with respect to the order in which communion would be distributed and the methodology of delivery.

Order of Communion Distribution

Throughout Church history, there seems to be a variety of practices, with respect to the order in which members would receive communion – whether by rank, gender, marital status, or season of life. I will highlight three distinct practices, including instructions given in the Apostolic Constitution in the fourth century, the Alexandrian practice in thirteenth to fifteenth century Egypt, and contemporary practices found in the Coptic Orthodox Church.

One of the earliest written instructions about communion order comes from the Apostolic Constitutions (380 AD). During that time period, there appears a clear instruction that outlines each of the ranks and the order in which they ought to commune:

> Let the bishop communicate, then the presbyters and the deacons and the subdeacons and the readers and the cantors and the ascetics and, from among the women, the deaconesses and the virgins and the widows, then the children, and finally all the people, in order.[27]

During the time of Pope Cyril III ibn Laqlaq (1235-1243),

---

[27] *The Apostolic Constitution*, vol. VIII, 13:14 380AD.

The Book of the Guide[28] mentions that "the presiding priest gives communion even to the bishops in attendance at the service, except in the case of the local diocesan, who precedes even the presiding celebrant in giving himself communion."[29] Approximately 150 years later during the time of Pope Gabriel V (1409-1427), the same practice is reiterated in the patriarchal work entitled *Liturgical Order.*[30]

Modern Coptic communion practices have certain variations that are quite clearly different from earlier periods. Distribution almost universally begins with the highest ranking clergy serving the Body and the Blood first to himself followed by other participating clergy including bishops, priests, deacons, and then all of the other diaconal ranks together who are present in the sanctuary. Although in theory, one might expect that communion distribution would follow to the various diaconal ranks in proper order, in reality and in practice I have never witnessed such a distinction. Rather, all members of the various diaconal ranks are then administered the sacrament without distinction. In conclusion the men and then the women are communed, although in some cases children will be communed prior to adults.

Methodology of Communion Delivery

Many of the faithful today might be under the impression that the current methodology of administering communion is the 'traditional' manner in which the Church has always distributed the

---

[28] A sort of rubric for liturgical celebrants found in codex *Vatican Arabic 117.*

[29] Robert Taft, "Byzantine Communion Rites: The Early Ritual of Clergy Communion," *OCP*, no. 65 (1999): 307–45, 322.

[30] Ibid.

sacrament. However, I will provide a few examples that will highlight the fact that there has been a diversity of practices when it comes to the distribution of communion throughout various time periods.

During the fourth Century, St. Cyril of Jerusalem instructs those recently catechized into the Church with the proper way in which they should receive the Eucharist directly in their hand. He instructs recent initiates: "in approaching therefore, come not with your wrists extended, or your fingers spread; but make your left hand a throne for the right, as for that which is to receive a King. And having hollowed your palm, receive the Body of Christ, saying over it, Amen." [31] In addition to Cyril's emphasis on a certain methodology, he is also highlighting the importance of approaching the King in a reverent manner.

Near the end of the fourth century, the laity and desert hermits in Egypt were instructed to commune themselves at home:

> For once the priest has completed the sacrifice and distributed [communion], the one who received it [i.e., his entire weekly ration of the Eucharistic gifts] all at once, should reasonably believe that when he received it each day [at home], he is receiving and communicating from the one who gave it to him [at the liturgy]. [32]

Some scholars suggest that St. Basil of Caesarea's *letter 93* should be properly understood within its proper context, as during a period of persecution in Egypt. Basil seeks to assure the faithful that they were not committing any fault through participating in such an unfamiliar practice, as they were in exceptional times and due to the extreme

---

[31] Cyril of Jerusalem, *Catechetical Lectures*, vol. XXI, 350AD.

[32] Taft, "Byzantine Communion Rites: The Early Ritual of Clergy Communion", 313.

circumstances. [33] Moreover, in the fifth century, St. Shenouda—Abbot of Egypt's White Monastery and author of a revered Coptic corpus of writings on monasticism and praxis—instructed his monks to receive communion in their hands. The early twentieth century Liturgist Reginald Maxwell Woolley uncovered manuscripts documenting sixteenth century Coptic practices where "the Communion is given in both species at once, the Consecrated Bread being slightly dipped in the chalice and placed in the communicant's mouth, sometimes by means of a spoon."[34] Finally, the modern method of sacramental distribution is given for the majority of members by the priest placing the Consecrated Bread (the Holy Body) directly into the open mouth of communicants followed by distributing the Consecrated Wine (the Precious Blood) through a shared spoon.

In no way am I proposing a complete change to either the order of communion or the methodology of distribution. Rather, I am drawing attention to historical precedence for a diversity of practices. In contrast to those who argue that this current practice is 'the traditional' way in which the Eucharist has always been distributed, history highlights for us that the contemporary means simply fall within a tradition of diversity, which acknowledged the unchanging confession of the what (the Body and Blood of our Lord) and the why (for the salvation of our souls), while accepting a diversity in the how (the order and methodology of distribution). The goal of our lives is, after all, communion with God. This is the very reason why the Church never failed to find any means possible to distribute communion to the faithful, even in the midst of extreme circumstances. Furthermore, the Incarnation is the material and

---

[33] Ibid.

[34] Reginald Maxwell Woolley, *The Bread of the Eucharist* (London, UK: A.R. Mowbray & Co. Ltd., 1913), 47.

social reality of the hypostasis of the Son. As a result, the sacramental offering is made by material signs and physical presence, rather than just human life emulating Christ. In our current crisis where attendance in church is either unsafe, forbidden or limited, how might individuals make sense of living out their Christian vocation?

Chapter Two

Historical Response

T hroughout history, numerous situations have drastically impacted Church life. In some cases, extensive changes may have been the result of natural occurrences (i.e. plagues or famines) while other times the impacts were clearly due to corrupt human activity (persecution). In this chapter, I will give an overview of a variety of plagues, famines, and periods of persecution that have affected church life. Whereas, the following is not intended to be an exhaustive list of each category, it will certainly shed light on historical precedents from which we can draw lessons for today. Although one may question why there is a necessity to look at famines and periods of persecution, especially during times of a pandemic, I believe that in light of the drastic circumstances of the COVID-19 crisis, it will be useful to learn from situations which deeply impacted how people lived out their lives and when the Church adapted to her current climate. Whether it was through responding to the theological and spiritual questions, liturgical considerations, or social necessities during the times of the plagues, famines, and periods of persecution, the lessons from the past will be useful as the Church seeks to contextualize within a Coronavirus world.

I.   *Plagues*

There have been numerous outbreaks and epidemics that have profoundly impacted human life and caused extreme suffering and countless deaths. These plagues understandably also impacted church life, specifically liturgical practices and funeral services. Some of the more well-known cases include Galen's plague, the Cyprian Plague, and the Great Plague.

Galen's Plague

Between 165-180 AD, a smallpox epidemic struck Asia minor and much of Europe, leading to the death of roughly five million people, including two Roman emperors. The plague is sometimes referred to as the Galen plague, named after the famous Roman physician. Others refer to it as the Antonine plague, named after the well-known Roman emperor Marcus Aurelius Antoninus who died as a result of the plague. This plague is believed to have begun amongst soldiers on the eastern frontiers of the empire and spread rapidly upon the return of the infected soldiers to Rome in 166.[35] Dio Cassius, an ancient historian, "estimated that the disease was killing 2,000 [persons] a day in the city of Rome at its height, with as many as four times that being infected."[36] Although fear mounted and many

---

[35] R. S. Bray, *Armies of Pestilence: The Impact of Disease on History* (James Clarke & Co., 2004), 12.

[36] Jerry Toner, *Roman Disasters* (John Wiley & Sons, 2018), 26.

Romans blamed Christians for making the gods angry and thus triggering the outbreak, Christians remained unwavering in their faith to God and service to their neighbors. Unlike pagan physicians like Galen who fled the plague in Rome for his country estate, the Christian presbyters and deacons courageously and faithfully served the sick, with many of them even sacrificing their own lives in the process.[37] As a result of such distinguishing acts of sacrificial service, Christianity spread rapidly throughout the empire at the end of the second century.

Cyprian's Plague

Between 252-266 AD, while the world was still recovering from the Galen plague, another outbreak occurred. This time it is believed that the plague was either related to measles or smallpox once again. Striking much of the Mediterranean region, this devastating plague claimed the lives of nearly 5,000 people each day in Rome and seems to have hit the rural areas as hard as the cities.[38] The plague is named after Cyprian, the Bishop of Carthage, due to his influence during this time period and the descriptive text he left in his work *On Mortality.* Cyprian describes the symptoms of the plague in the following manner:

> That now the bowels loosened into a flux exhaust the strength of the body, that a fever contracted in the very marrow of the bones breaks out into ulcers of the throat, that the intestines are shaken by continual vomiting, that the blood-shot eyes burn, that the feet of some or certain parts of their members are cut away by the infection of

---

[37] Rodney Stark, *The Triumph of Christianity: How the Jesus Movement Became the World's Largest Religion* (New York: Harper One, 2011), 116-119.

[38] Princeton Review, *Cracking the AP World History Exam, 2018 Edition* (Random House Children's Books, 2017), 508.

diseased putrefaction, that, by a weakness developing through the losses and injuries of the body, either the gait is enfeebled, or the hearing impaired, or the sight blinded.[39]

Although Christians were not shielded from the devastation caused by the plague, Cyprian reminded them that "many of us are dying in this mortality…as to the fact that, without any discrimination in the human race, the just also are dying with the unjust."[40] Without trying to give justification why, Cyprian simply affirms to the Christians that such a ravenous disease does not discriminate based on faith. Humanity continues to be susceptible to such attacks on the flesh due to the Fall, and irrespective of one's faithfulness to God. In other words, he is reminding Christians that they do not receive some special privilege of protection against this plague.

Meanwhile Cyprian's plague spread well beyond Rome to Egypt. With some calculations suggesting that two-thirds of the population of Alexandria may have perished, St. Dionysius, bishop of Alexandria, spoke of the impact of the plague in his region. The following is an excerpt from a fragment of one of Dionysius' Festal letters that has been preserved in Eusebius' *Church History*:

> This pestilence has overtaken us, which is to them a more fearful thing than all former fears and more terrible than any calamity whatever, and to quote an expression of an historian of their own, "a thing which alone has exceeded all men's expectation," while to us it was not so much that as a discipline and a testing no less severe than any of the rest: for it did not spare us, though it attacked the Gentiles in great force.[41]

---

[39] Cyprian of Carthage, *On Mortality*, 14.

[40] Ibid, 15.

[41] Eusebius of Caesarea, *Church History*, vol. 7, 22.

CHURCH LIFE IN A CORONAVIRUS WORLD
The Great Plague

In 2013, researchers confirmed that the bacteria *Yersinia pestis,* responsible for the Great Plague of 1347-1351, was also the cause of the earlier Justinian plague of the sixth century.[42] Although this epidemic spanned just a few years, it too ravaged the known world at the time, killing an estimated one-third to one-half of the population throughout Eurasia and North Africa. Claiming the lives of between 75 million to 200 million people, the Great Plague decimated the known world. History has documented how Christians in Europe and in North Africa, including Egypt, responded to the great plague.

One well known story is about a fourteenth century Catholic missionary named Roch, the son of the mayor of Montpelier. Roch traveled throughout Italy serving those who had been infected with bubonic plague. Ultimately becoming sick from exposure, he died from the plague as well. Later canonized as a saint by the Catholic Church, Roch served as an example of Christ-like sacrifice for other Christians in Europe during times of plague.

The situation in Egypt was different, the Church sought to make modifications to its funeral services since it is estimated that hundreds of people were dying daily in the streets of Alexandria alone, following the arrival of the plague in the fall of 1347. As the Great Plague spread throughout Egypt in less than a year, it is believed that more than a third of the 600,000 residents died there. Historians have argued that over the next 150 years, the plague

---

[42] "Modern Lab Reaches across the Ages to Resolve Plague DNA Debate," accessed May 8, 2020, https://phys.org/news/2013-05-modern-lab-ages-plague-dna.html.

returned to Cairo more than 50 times, ravaging the population.[43] As a result of the innumerable amount of graves needing to be dug for all of the corpses, the funeral rite of the general funeral service was introduced following the Palm Sunday service. Anyone who died during Pascha week would be immediately buried and considered to have been prayed upon. Edward William Lane, a 19th century British historian, further documented that "priests recite the prayers of the dead over their congregations in the churches; and if any die between that day and the end of the Khamaseen[44] (which is the chief or worst portion of the plague-season), his body is interred without the prayer being repeated. This custom seems to have originated from the fact of its being impossible to pray at the tomb over every victim of the plague; and must have a very impressive effect upon people expecting the dreadful scourge."[45]

II. *Famines*

During times of great famine, when people are unable to provide food for their families, many of the faithful sacrificed their faith, turning their attention to temporal survival, seeking any means possible of providing one of the most basic human needs. In this next section I will highlight some of the famines that occurred during the time of Coptic Christianity in Egypt and how the Christians responded during these various times. Due to the limited information

---

[43] Joseph Patrick Byrne, *Encyclopedia of the Black Death* (ABC-CLIO, 2012), 65-66.

[44] Although the *General Funeral Service* rite at one point extended from Palm Sunday through the "Khamaseen"—a transliterated word from Arabic describing the 50 Days following Resurrection—the current practice covers only during Pascha week from Palm Sunday through the Feast of Resurrection.

[45] Edward William Lane, *An Account of the Manners and Customs of the Modern Egyptians* (John Murray, 1860), 541.

currently available, I will simply provide a listing of some of the famines with few details, to provide perspective for the reader as to how the Christians responded to the increased funeral services, provided for social needs of the destitute, and theologically understood their circumstances.

Pope Benjamin I, 38th Patriarch (623-662)

At the time Pope Benjamin, a deadly famine arose, which wiped out so many people that the dead were thrown in the streets and by the Nile in such large quantities that some described the scene as resembling a 'fish market.'[46] As the faithful could not find anybody to bury them because of the high number of daily funerals, they began to perform mass burials simultaneously. Whereas it was the custom of the Church not to perform a funeral on Sunday, there were also accommodations made to allow for funerals during that time on Sunday's.[47]

Pope James, 50th Patriarch (819-830)

As a famine arose in the ninth century during the time of Pope James, he was unable to provide meals and assistance for the churches and the destitute amongst them. Nothing was left to the patriarchate due to the mismanagement of funds by Pope James's predecessor coupled with the severity of the famine. In addition, the pilgrimages by the faithful to the church of the martyr Saint Menas at Maryût were interrupted for several years, as well as with those who

---

[46] "History of the Patriarchs: Deir Al-Syrian Edition," Part 1, 121.

[47] Ibid.

used to travel to Alexandria to trade with the patriarchate.[48] Although no positive response was taken during this time of famine, I chose to include it as a reference point for how mismanagement of resources impacted the Church during times of unexpected hardship, when decisive action was needed.

Pope Joseph, 52nd Patriarch (830-849)

The *History of the Patriarchs* documents the hyperinflation that occurred during the famine at the time of Pope Joseph. Such economic peril, coupled with the famine, led to "many of the women and infants and young people, and of the old and the middle-aged, [dying] of starvation...due to the severity of the famine."[49] Further compounding the crisis, the person who oversaw the collection of taxes was also intentionally harming the people by driving up taxes so high that some of the people – in their great distress – even sold their own children in order to pay their taxes.[50] Of particular interest for the context of this paper, and with reference to some people's theological inquiry about the source of such crisis – the people did not see the famine as an act of anger from God, but rather an act of mercy and righteousness.[51] Their belief was that God is loving and good and provides all that is needed for the sake of their healing. This, of course, was seen in contrast to the wicked deeds of the tax collector who was seeking to drive people deeper into bondage.

During the various times of famine, the Church not only

---

[48] Severus of Al'Ashmunein (Hermopolis), *History of the Patriarchs of the Coptic Church of Alexandria: Part 4: Mennas I - Joseph (849 AD).*, vol. 10 (Patrologia Orientalis, 1910), Chapter 19.

[49] Ibid, Chapter 20.

[50] Ibid.

[51] Ibid.

sought to respond to the social needs of the people by providing meals and financial support, but also was prepared to modify funeral services due to the tragic reality the people lived in; she did all of this with a proper theological paradigm. The Christians believed that what happened through the natural and created order was a result of God's ongoing act of love. Simultaneously they recognized each moment as an opportunity to lovingly serve one another. Although we are not in the midst of a famine at the time of writing this book, I wonder if there will be an aftermath of economic crisis in which Christians may need to take action and plan for mitigating the financial and food crisis that their brothers and sisters – and humanity at-large – might face.[52]

III. *Persecutions*

One may question the rationale for addressing persecution in a work that seeks to provide a response to the COVID-19 pandemic. Although the conditions are not identical, there are several valuable lessons to learn from how the Church responded during exceptional times of crisis. As Christians found themselves unable to worship and practice their faith freely (liturgical services were oftentimes banned and significant limitations were placed upon Christians), I believe the concepts will speak to the hearts of many faithful today. There have been at least two dozen waves of persecution in Christian history that lead to required modifications in Church life. I will address six of the more extreme periods of persecution that the Coptic Orthodox church in Egypt endured and will relate lessons for consideration. It is important to note that I am not suggesting that the limitations on

---

[52] Abdi Latif Dahir, "'Instead of Coronavirus, the Hunger Will Kill Us.' A Global Food Crisis Looms. - The New York Times," April 22, 2020, https://www.nytimes.com/2020/04/22/world/africa/coronavirus-hunger-crisis.html.

Church services during the COVID-19 pandemic are a form of religious persecution. Rather, I am pointing to how Christians responded to situations when their Church life was restricted.

Pope Theonas, 16ᵗʰ Patriarch (282-300)

At the end of the third century, a great wave of persecution fell upon the Church in Egypt at the time of the Roman Emperor Diocletian. Although Christians were banned from worshipping Jesus Christ, they did not allow such an imperial edict to prevent them from remaining faithful to God. During the time of Pope Theonas, the faithful – being forced into hiding – prayed, engaged in time of worship, received communion, and baptized children and adults in caves, mountains, homes and other hidden places. This period lasted for several years, as the Christians feared severe attacks from unbelievers.[53] Although 'churches were closed', this did not prevent Christians from being creative about locating alternative places and finding other means to worship God and commune with Him.

Pope Peter I, 17ᵗʰ Patriarch (300-311)

The successor of Theonas, Pope Peter I[54] served at an unusually turbulent time in the early history of the Church. Defending the faith against false teaching and opposing the edicts of the two emperors Diocletian and Maximin Daia – who forbade Christian services – Pope Peter was a great "advocate of leniency and terms of penance for those Christians who paid homage to the pagan

---

[53] *Coptic Synaxarium*, vol. 2, 78.

[54] Pope Peter 1 is traditionally referred to as the seal of the martyrs, as he was one of the final martyrs during the reign of Diocletian and preceding Emperor Constantine's Edict of Milan in 312 legalizing Christianity.

gods after Diocletian's edict of 303."[55] The temperament of Pope Peter is to be commended, especially at a time when some of his contemporaries were quick to judge the faith of the lapsed[56] members and to exclude them from communion within the Church.

Pope Theodosius, 33rd Patriarch (535-566)

At a time when conflict in Egypt raged between the Coptic Orthodox Christians and the Byzantine Empire, Pope Theodosius I was exiled by an imperial decree. Although, Menas – the Byzantine bishop of Constantinople – attempted to ordain a new bishop for Alexandria, the Copts refused to accept him. When the Byzantine prince learned of the refusal of the Christians in Alexandria to accept his decision, he became enraged and "commanded that the doors of the churches in the city of Alexandria should be shut and sealed with his seal, and guards set before them, so that no one at all might enter." Although the people were deeply saddened by this decision, "they remained in this condition for a whole year, without communion, or a church to pray in, or a place to be baptized in."[57]

Pope Isaac, the 41st Patriarch (686-689)

The successor of Pope John III, who served during the time of a ravenous famine (mentioned in the previous section), Pope Isaac was confronted with a different type of danger following an incident

---

[55] Donald Spanel and Tim Vivian, "Peter I," in *The Coptic Encyclopedia*, ed. Aziz S. Atiya (Claremont, 1991).

[56] The term 'lapsed' refers to a person who either temporarily or permanently ceased following the faith of the Church.

[57] Severus of Al'Ashmunein (Hermopolis), *History of the Patriarchs of the Coptic Church of Alexandria: Peter I - Benjamin I (661 AD). Pp. 383-518 (Pp.119-256 of Text).*, vol. 2 (Patrologia Orientalis, 1904), https://www.ccel.org/ccel/pearse/morefathers/files/severus_hermopolis_his t_alex_patr_02_part2.htm#THEODOSIUS_I.

related to international politics:

> Isaac mediated between the emperor of Ethiopia and the Christian king of Nubia, who were in conflict at the time. Apparently, this infuriated 'Abd al-Aziz [the Arab governor of Egypt], who put the patriarch under house arrest in Alexandria to prevent him from crossing the frontier to the African potentates with whom Egypt was not in harmony. But curiously his fury went beyond the patriarch to the whole of the Coptic church, and the governor ordered all crosses, even gold and silver ones, to be broken from churches. Furthermore, he issued an order that posters should be fixed on the gates of all churches bearing the inscription that Muhammad is the apostle of Allah and that Jesus is only the prophet of God and not his son, for Allah is neither born nor bearing.[58]

This period of persecution lasted for three years, in which the 64 Coptic bishops were also placed on house arrest and all Eucharistic celebrations were banned. Once again, this did not prevent the Copts from remaining faithful to Christ, as they continued to pray in their homes, remaining committed to His Church, until they could once again assemble together.

Pope Cosmas II, 54th Patriarch (852-856)

During a time of fierce oppression in Egypt, Pope Cosmas II faced an unusual decision. Abd al-Masih ibn Ishaq, an appointee by the Caliph, decided to impose extreme measures against the Church, which included imposing severe financial demands, restrictions on ringing of bells, and the requirement that all crosses on churches were to be broken. Perhaps none of these was quite the gut punch that came next, as "the sale of wine was prohibited in order to deprive the priesthood of the use of sacramental wine. In response, Christians would procure grapevines, soak them in water, and press them for

---

[58] Subhi Labib and Aziz S. Atiya, "Isaac," in *The Coptic Encyclopedia* (Claremont, 1991).

juice as a substitute to the wine in the celebration of the Liturgy."[59] In order for the Church to continue providing Eucharistic liturgies for the faithful, a great deal of creativity and flexibility was required by the leadership. Although this was the first recorded event when the Coptic Church utilized a different substance than wine in the Eucharistic offering, this did not prevent them from doing so. The faithful understood the principle that the 'what' and the 'why' were unnegotiable, but that accommodations could be made with the 'how,' especially during exceptional times.

Pope Zacharias, 64th Patriarch (1003-1032)

The period of the Fatimids remains one of the most extraordinarily difficult times for the Christians of Egypt. Of particular interest, for the scope of this work, was the period of Al-ḥākim Bi-amr Allāh, the sixth Caliph of the Fatimid Empire. In addition to banning the Festal Celebration of Resurrection[60] and forbidding the use of wine for Church services in 1004,[61] the caliph also enacted a nine year period of extreme tribulation during which Eucharistic celebrations were forbidden. Whereas the priests initially attempted to travel to homes with the 'holy tablet' to celebrate the Eucharist, baptisms and marriages when possible, some manuscripts suggest that liturgies almost ceased entirely in Egypt outside the monasteries. Priests entering homes for liturgical celebrations were oftentimes discovered, arrested, and imprisoned. Since the believers were accustomed to living the liturgical life as a family, a great many

---

[59] Subhi Labib and Aziz S. Atiya, "Cosmas," in *The Coptic Encyclopedia* (Claremont, 1991).

[60] Robert Ousterhout, "Rebuilding the Temple: Constantine Monomachus and the Holy Sepulchre," *The Journal of the Society of Architectural Historians* 48, no. 1 (March 1989): 66–78.

[61] *The Druze in the Middle East: Their Faith, Leadership, Identity and Status* (Brighton England ; Portland, Or: Sussex Academic Press, 2003).

of them resorted to praying the liturgy of the Word at home.[62] As this continued for several years, one might consider the various ways in which the Christians must have been negatively impacted as a result of this unfortunate event. A well-known account amongst Copts suggests that one day as the Caliph was walking through Cairo on a Sunday morning during the usual time of Divine Liturgy for the Christians, he heard prayers coming from hundreds of homes. In that moment, he realized that his intention of closing the churches had back-fired. In fact, his action led to the conversion of every home into a church. As a result, he immediately ordered that all churches should be re-opened.

In conclusion, I will restate that the intention of highlighting such details about persecution is not for the purposes of scandalizing certain persons or groups for their actions against the Christians, but to rather highlight the creativity, determination, and flexibility of the Copts when they were faced with such extreme circumstances.

During times of imminent mortality, humans have a tendency to consider and reflect upon their matters of faith. Whether in responding to extraordinary circumstances at times of plagues, famine, or extreme periods of persecution, the Christians of Egypt always remained faithful to their primary focus. Deeply concerned with remaining in union with God, serving the Christian population, and being a light in the world, the Copts – led by the Holy Spirit – persisted in creativity and flexibility on form, while at the same time never letting go of the essence, even in the face of imminent death. If churches were closed, the priest would go to the houses. If the priests were forbidden from doing so, the people would pray the liturgy of the Word in their homes. When wine was banned from being utilized, they soaked grapevines in water and utilized the extracted

---

[62] Source: *Biography of the Holy Church according to the Ancient Manuscripts: Study and Analysis, Sherif Ramzy. (In print, forthcoming);a researched of ecclesial history.*

juice instead. Always focused on the present reality of Christ in their midst, they did not allow a change in location, modification in materials, or their own personal discomfort to impact their commitment as Christians living in the midst of a broken world.

Whether it was through addressing the theological and spiritual questions, liturgical considerations, or social necessities during the times of these of plagues, famines, or periods of persecution, the Church never strayed from the essence of the faith, while at the same time maintaining a tradition of diversity. This ultimately allowed her to respond not only to the challenges before her, but to continue to grow following times of great crisis.

Chapter Three

Recommendations

The collective tradition of how the Church historically dealt with various catastrophes – similar to the COVID-19 crisis – sheds light on how to encounter a season of pandemic. Rather than seeing our current situation as a moment to fear, withdraw or complain, Christians must learn from their ancestors of faith in order to engage with the crisis of the present moment; not as the world is doing, but as ambassadors of Christ. In order to do so, I believe Christians today must follow the same consistent methodology seen throughout every era of the Church. With a need to be creative about reaching people for the sake of their salvation in Christ, the Church should be less fixated during the current crisis on the 'how,' while remaining unwavering on the 'what' and the 'why'. It is clear from Church history that she has always understood the necessity of diversity (how) in presenting Christ to others (what) for the sake of their salvation (why). Based on the research, I have distilled three areas that require a response by the Church today. These include: provision for theological and spiritual answers, liturgical considerations, and social necessities.

Theological and Spiritual Answers

One of the clear distinguishing factors between Christians and their counterparts during past times of plagues, famines, and persecutions was in how they viewed and responded to their current crisis. Frequently in human history, tragedies produced by natural or social disasters resulted in a crisis of faith for many people. However, some of the insights and demeanors of Christians were so compelling to pagans and other non-believers that many non-Christians were drawn to Christ in the midst of, and following, these terrible times.

Although Christians did not always seek to provide a definitive answer to explain the cause of the devastation, there does seem to be an allowance for a variety of explanations. Early Christians were quite comfortable accepting their limited capacity to fully comprehend why God was doing or allowing certain events. Therefore, they often avoided trying to be the 'mouthpiece of God' by providing definitive and declarative statements which seemed to interpret their current circumstances from a divinely motivated perspective. Such language and approach does not seem to become mainstream until the time of medieval European theology[63] when plagues are seen in light of eschatological terms.[64] Prior to that, it is

---

[63] "Reactions to Plague in the Ancient & Medieval World," Ancient History Encyclopedia, accessed May 14, 2020, https://www.ancient.eu/article/1534/reactions-to-plague-in-the-ancient--medieval-world/.

[64] Brian David Yurochko, "Cultural and Intellectual Responses to the Black Death" (Electronic Theses and Dissertations, Duquesne University, 2009), 94-96. Yurochko highlights the correlation medieval European theologians

suffice to say that, Christians seemed comfortable emphasizing theological reality rather than trying to squeeze specific events into a certain paradigm. Since paganism and Hellenic philosophies – similar to modern day secularism – was able to provide no existential explanation, people turned to Christianity, with its focus on divine realism rather than temporality.

As Adam willfully turned away from God, he deprived his created nature of the life-sustaining grace of God. This resulted in the human soul experiencing death, likewise infecting the human body with disease and mortality. In like manner, the entire cosmos became disrupted, further perpetuating disease throughout the world. St. Athanasius of Alexandria states that, as a result of the Fall, "men began to die, while corruption thence-forward prevailed against them, gaining even more than its natural power over the whole race."[65] Death is therefore neither a revenge nor punishment from an angry God, but rather a natural result of humanity's willful turning away from Life. [66] However, the Lord—not desiring to leave humanity in this fallen condition out of His perpetual love for humankind—was incarnate, uniting Himself to humanity for the sake of our salvation. Extending His hands on the cross, He signified His desire to draw all humanity to Himself [67] with the final nail in the coffin for death coming through the Resurrection of Christ from the

---

made between the current circumstances of plague and political upheaval with the reign of Antichrist and the end of the world. They interpreted certain eschatological events through the lens of wrath, along with language in Revelation that appears to be distinct from earlier Christian literature.

[65] Athanasius of Alexandria, *On the Incarnation*, trans. John Behr (Yonkers, NY: St. Vladimir's Seminary Press, 2011), 5.

[66] Corinna Delkeskamp-Hayes, "Why Patients Should Give Thanks for Their Disease: Traditional Christianity on the Joy of Suffering," *Christian Bioethics* 12, no. 2 (August 1, 2006): 213–28, 216.

[67] Athanasius of Alexandria, *On the Incarnation*, 25.

dead. The last enemy had been conquered with Christians now joyfully greeting one another with the words of victory "Christ is Risen; Truly He is Risen!"[68]

What made Christianity truly compelling though was not simply one theological argument over another, but the spiritual dimension of a living faith by countless Christians. St. Paul the Apostle wrote about the power of a life well-lived in Christ when he said, "You are our epistle written in our hearts, known and read by all men; clearly you are an epistle of Christ, ministered by us, written not with ink but by the Spirit of the living God, not on tablets of stone but on tablets of flesh, that is, of the heart."[69] As living epistles of Christ, Christians were committed to living their vocation as disciples of Jesus. This was clearly seen during the third century Cyprian plague, when Christians witnessed with their lives to the meaningfulness of life even amidst sudden death. In *On Mortality*, Cyprian of Carthage writes:

> What greatness of soul it is to fight with the powers of the mind unshaken against so many attacks of devastation and death, what sublimity to stand erect amidst the ruins of the human race and not to lie prostrate with those who have no hope in God, and to rejoice rather and embrace the gift of the occasion, which, while we are firmly expressing our faith, and having endured sufferings, are advancing to Christ by the narrow way of Christ, we should receive as the reward of His way and faith, He himself being our judge! Let him certainly be afraid to die who, not having been reborn of water and the spirit is delivered up to the fires of hell. Let him be afraid to die who is not listed under the cross and passion of Christ.

[68] It is customary within the Orthodox Church to greet one another with the Resurrectional salutation "Christ is Risen" with a response of "Truly He is Risen." This greeting amongst the faithful lasts for fifty days from the Feast of Resurrection until the Feast of Pentecost.

[69] 2 Corinthians 3:2-3.

Let him be afraid to die who will pass from this death to a second death.[70]

As a message to the Christians of Carthage, Cyprian is both invoking a word of encouragement to continue to live with endurance in the face of the plague they are confronted by, while at the same time using a rhetorical style of writing to remind the Christians they have nothing to fear. He continues to describe how the Christians almost appeared to pursue martyrdom due to their utter absence of fear for death:

> Although this mortality has contributed nothing else, it has especially accomplished this for Christians and servants of God, that we have begun gladly to seek martyrdom while we are learning not to fear death. These are trying exercises for us, not deaths; they give to the mind the glory of fortitude; by contempt of death they prepare for the crown...our brethren who have been freed from the world by the summons of the Lord should not be mourned, since we know that they are not lost but sent before; that in departing they lead the way; that as travelers, as voyagers are wont to be, they should be longed for, not lamented...and that no occasion should be given to pagans to censure us deservedly and justly, on the ground that we grieve for those who we say are living with God.[71]

For those who died as a result of the smallpox plague, Cyprian reminded them that they had nothing to fear and everything to gain. As St. Paul says, "For to me, to live is Christ, and to die is gain."[72] He admonishes the Christians that even the way in which they respond to the departure of loved ones from this world is an opportune time to testify to their faith in the living God. Cyprian continues by reminding the faithful that those who have passed on from this world

---

[70] Cyprian of Carthage, *On Mortality, 14.*

[71] Ibid, 16, 20.

[72] Philippians 1:21.

are not dead but have simply departed:

> For believing in Christ's resurrection we also believe in
> our own, for it was for us that he died and rose again. And
> so since the resurrection of the dead is established, there
> is no room for grief at death...For why grieve if you do
> not believe that a person has perished? Why should you
> be impatient that someone has been stolen away for a
> while when you believe that he will return? What you
> take to be death is merely a departure. He who goes
> before you is not to be mourned but simply missed. And
> that sense of missing is to be tempered with patience; for
> why should you take it excessively badly that a person has
> gone away when you will soon follow?[73]

Even a shattered remnant of survivors who had somehow made it through war, plague, or both maintained a healing consolation in the vision of a heavenly existence for those missing relatives and friends who had departed this world. Whereas many of their neighbors lived in fear and despondency, the Christian courage, faithfulness, and joy in the face of plague became infectious to non-Christians, drawing countless others to Christ.

The non-Christian community was deeply impacted by the faith and life of their Christian neighbors. The idea that the Creator would be incarnate out of His desire for the salvation of the world was extremely different from the view of the philosophers, who understood 'God' as the unmoved mover unwilling to engage the world. The Christian understanding of God's love expressed on the cross was radically different from that of the bloodthirsty and angry pagan 'gods' in need of being appeased by human sacrifices. As Christians lived an authentic expression of their faith, many non-believers were compelled to come to Christ. Refusing to complain about their temporal circumstances, Christians lived with a hopeful, even enthusiastic, portrait of the future life; Christianity blossomed.

---

[73] Ibid, 31.

Christians today need to re-evaluate their response to the COVID-19 pandemic in light of the spiritual giants from previous generations.

Liturgical Life

There is possibly nothing more reflective of the values and identity of the Orthodox Christian Church than her liturgical worship. Since liturgy properly understood is 'the work of the people',[74] many people are rediscovering that Liturgy should not be understood as a presentation by a priest with a few deacons, but rather it is an activity of the entire congregation. Therefore, in the age of Zoom and YouTube, one must ask the question, 'is virtual church, fully church?' Whereas some may consider virtual church a substitute measure during these unique times, we must look ahead to the next season of life. Humans are creatures of habit and moments like these tend to redefine society and how we live out life. We must be intentional with a long-term vision in mind, even if it means short term discomfort. After all, nothing of value tends to come without sacrifice. In this section, I will provide recommendations, areas for further consideration, and questions for future discussion on a number of topics related to liturgical practices.

Families Building Liturgical Life at Home

Initially, during the first few weeks following the coronavirus pandemic global lockdown, countless prayer meetings, Bible studies, sermons, and liturgies were being streamed on-line. People tuned in around the clock consuming hours of 'spiritual content'. In some respects, this is certainly positive in that many people were seeking ways to remain connected to their faith, all while experiencing

---

[74] The Greek word for Liturgy means 'the work of the people.'

renewal through repentance. The question that I pondered was about the sustainability of such habits. For how long would people continue such habits? Would this lead to maturity in their Christian faith or could it contribute to an unhealthy dependency? Perhaps the issue was not in the services themselves, but in the emphasis and place of priority they were holding for some people. For the faithful to mature, such on-line content should only be considered as a supplement for what they are already doing at home. If Christians relied exclusively on this sort of content for their spiritual nourishment, it would have an adverse effect, preserving them in a state of spiritual infancy where they remain forever dependent on being spoon fed such materials. Just as in times past, when churches were closed for extended periods of time, Christians today must seek to develop their homes into churches. It is advisable that the faithful seek a rule of prayer from their Diocese or local church, with each person and family taking responsibility to maintain a spiritual rhythm in their home. This pattern of life would include daily time of reading the Bible, offering a sacrifice of praise, praying the hours, having quiet time, engaging in *Lectio Divina*, or sacred reading, examining oneself, and serving others in the home (and beyond, if possible). We should desire this season of the world to be likened to the time when St. Anthony entered the wilderness for years of retreat, after which when he returned to the world he descended upon it as a shining star illuminating the minds and hearts of those drawn to the Christ in him. Weeks into the coronavirus pandemic, we remain uncertain about what lies ahead. Let us consider that the foundation of the family altar in the home is that which has – and will – sustain the Christians during the numerous times of crisis when churches were closed for extended periods of time.

Private Liturgy

Although numerous liturgical celebrations have taken place in churches without congregations, I am not convinced that liturgical services must continue "under the current conditions [to] be served for the life of the world."[75] Although there has never been a time that the Eucharist has not be celebrated in the world by a community, as the monastic communities continued to celebrate Liturgy during times when the remaining Christians in a region were prevented from doing so, some fear that if the local church does not pray a Eucharistic liturgy that the sacrifice has been stopped. As the primary purpose of the Eucharist is to unite humanity as one family into the body of Christ, it is essential to examine current practices and popular thought on such matters. As Christians gather around the person of Jesus Christ – just as His disciples gathered around Him in His lifetime – we do so to experience and reflect *koinonia*.[76] Only if we hear Christ say – as He did at the Last Supper – "by this shall all men know that you are my disciples, that you love one another,"[77] that we may assert that liturgy has begun to be fulfilled with all those who are 'present,' as "Christian worship generally implies a community physically present in one place."[78] The issue thus is not in the small collection of people praying the Liturgy during times when

---

[75] Press Release, "The Church without the Eucharist Is Not the Church - Interview with John Zizioulas," *Anglican Ink © 2020* (blog), April 1, 2020, http://anglican.ink/2020/03/31/the-church-without-the-eucharist-is-not-the-church-interview-with-john-zizioulas/.

[76] *Koinonia* is a Greek word, commonly used in Christian communities, understood to be communion or fellowship with God and with other fellow members of the Church.

[77] John 13:35c.

CHURCH LIFE IN A CORONAVIRUS WORLD

gatherings must be limited, but rather the absence of realism that is reflected in the virtual church attempting to pray the Liturgy through online streaming.

To Stream or Not to Stream

Today you will find a full assortment of liturgical prayers streamed through various means to the faithful into their homes. Although this may appear to be a positive activity by the Church to reach the people using modern technological advances, there is an argument that not all services—due to their high level of sacredness—should be broadcast publicly. There are several eyewitnesses who claim that, during the years of his papacy, His Holiness Pope Kyrillos VI refused an offer made by the Egyptian government to stream the Divine Liturgy through the radio. Also, according to eyewitnesses, during the early years of the papacy of His Holiness Pope Shenouda, he upheld the same tradition by refusing to air the Liturgy of the faithful on public television. When asked about streaming the Liturgy during the COVID-19 pandemic, Archbishop John Zizoulous, modern Orthodox Christian theologian, stated that he does not "agree with the Divine Liturgy being transmitted by television. I'm confined to my home and will not be able to attend Liturgy. However, I will not turn the television on in order to watch the Liturgy. I consider that an expression of impiety. It is impious for someone to sit and watch the Liturgy."[79] That said, there are certainly times and forms of prayer which do not require a physical presence and that may be both suitable and beneficial for the Church.

---

[78] "Liturgy in a Time of Plague: A Letter to a Colleague," *Liturgy in a Time of Plague* (blog), accessed May 8, 2020, http://abmcg.blogspot.com/2020/03/liturgy-in-time-of-plague.html.

[79] Press Release, "The Church without the Eucharist Is Not the Church - Interview with John Zizioulas."

Furthermore, communal periods of fasting and prayer are nothing new and gathering for prayer meetings or Bible Study through technology has been around for decades. However, there is something antithetical to the practice of the Orthodox Church to stream the Liturgy of the Faithful.[80] This time of worship—preserved for the faithful who were gathered together in a single place—was to reflect their union with God and each other. In fact, the early Church would require non-baptized people to leave the Liturgy following the Gospel and sermon, after which the Eucharistic offering was made. Early Christians did not believe it fitting to 'cast pearls before' those who had not yet been baptized. Perhaps the solution during this time is not to suspend all streaming, but rather to only stream the Liturgy of the Word. After all, the Liturgy of the Word is intended to reveal the truth of Christ to the world through the reading of the scripture and preaching the Gospel.

Eucharistic Accommodations

During the time of the COVID-19 pandemic, there has been much rhetoric spewed by various groups of people about the role of worship services within a coronavirus world, with different factions accusing one another. There are, of course, those who consider themselves 'faithful' and others who consider themselves 'scientifically-minded':

---

[80] The Divine Liturgy in the Orthodox Church is a combination of the *Liturgy of the Word* followed by the *Liturgy of the Faithful*. The *Liturgy of the Word* includes the reading of scripture, the singing of various hymns, and a sermon. The *Liturgy of the Faithful* is the core of the Orthodox Eucharistic service.

- **"Faithful people"**: The self-proclaimed "faithful people" claim they have little (to no) fear when it comes to COVID-19, or any other risk for that matter, thereby ignoring historical evidence showing transfer of disease during communion,[81] or times when Christians were killed in churches during times of persecution. This group tends to thrive when the cost is greatest. If you asked them, they would say with conviction that they are *ready to die for the sake of Jesus today!* They tend to rush and categorize the 'others' as being fearful and unfaithful to God. Some of them have gone so far as to suggest that if one has any fears about getting infected during Church service, they are in some way approaching the Eucharistic table to eat or drink in an unworthy manner and are thus eating and drinking judgment unto themselves.[82] However, the Eucharist at its core is a medicine for those who are broken, not a trophy for those who are strong. Christ the Physician came for the diseased, not the healthy.

- **"Scientific-minded people"**: Then there are the so-called "scientific-minded people," who tend to put a greater emphasis on the visible. They like to think of themselves as being more intellectually minded than others. One of the dangers for this group is that they may look to the "faithful people" as being reckless, irresponsible, and backwards. This group may also be so captivated by the tangible aspects of this

---

[81] Although there were incidents where communion resulted in the death of the Abu-makar monks after the wine was poisoned before the liturgy. See Rafik Adel and Fr. Michael Al-Baramousi, "Preserving the Eucharistic Bread and the Rite of Reconstructing the Chalice," *Alexandria School Journal*, no. 21 (February 2016): 123–45.

[82] 1 Corinthians 11:28-30.

world that they forget they are living in the joy of the age to come.

Neither of these groups are fully reflective of the early Christian approach. Remember Pope Peter, the seal of the martyrs, who understood the need for leniency for those who struggled – not so much with their faith – but in the face of being killed for their faith, while he himself was being prepared to become a martyr.

Church history shows a community of people seeking various ways to save a broken humanity that was in the midst of repeated seasons of devastation. With respect to the Eucharist, Orthodox Christians understood that they could be flexible in the 'how' (the manner in which communion was distributed) while remaining unwavering on the 'what' (giving the Body and Blood of Christ) or the 'why' (for the sake of their salvation). In the words of St. Paul, they "have become all things to all people so that by all possible means [they] might save some."[83] When the Church throughout the ages modified communion distribution[84] – which included having a deacon provide the Eucharistic offering to those who are present and absent,[85] placing the Eucharist into the hands of the faithful, placing the Eucharist on a napkin in the hands of the communicant, providing communion for people to take throughout the week in their homes, or dipping the Body into the Blood and then placing into the mouth of the individual – they were not being unfaithful in

---

[83] 1 Corinthians 9:22.

[84] For a detailed research on the development of the communion distribution rite, highlighting early Christian writings and extensive Coptic manuscripts, the following article may be read in Arabic. Rafik Adel and Fr. Misael Al-Baramousi, "Preserving the Eucharistic Bread and the Rite of Reconstructing the Chalice," *Alexandria School Journal*, no. 21 (February 2016): 123–45.

[85] Justin Martyr, *Apology*, vol. 1, 65-67.

their belief in God or uncommitted to the Orthopraxy they had received. Perhaps there will be a time in the near future when the Church will need to learn from the various communion methods of the past or that she may even be required to possess the creativity of Pope Cosmas II, who was forced to soak grapevines in water and press them for juice as a substitute to the wine in celebration of the Liturgy.

Although the Church has historically modified her distribution practices due to the needs of the time, I urge the reader to be mindful of government interventions attempting to regulate aspects of Church life that is essential to her faith. The CDC's issued guidance to congregations that practice communion is to "consider modifying or suspending this practice." [86] Although the CDC's recommended modification of "placing the Communion elements in the recipient's hand...and [to avoid] use of a common cup"[87] does not conflict within the historical tradition of the Church, the greater concern is the recommendation to also consider suspending the practice of communion. I urge the reader to cautiously observe governmental attempts to restrict or force the faithful to suspend a practice that falls within the category of the essence of the faith, rather than one that may be reduced to a modifiable form.

Even if judgmental thoughts, critical attitudes, and divisive language is the norm of the world, it is imperative that Christians

---

[86] CDC, "Coronavirus Disease 2019 (COVID-19) - Get Your Community- and Faith-Based Organizations Ready for Coronavirus Disease 2019," Centers for Disease Control and Prevention, February 11, 2020, https://www.cdc.gov/coronavirus/2019-ncov/community/organizations/guidance-community-faith-organizations.html.

[87] Ibid.

avoid such behavior, which will only lead to greater loss. There is another way! One of Jesus' disciples said to Him "'Master, we saw someone casting out demons in Your name, and we forbade him because he does not follow with us.' But Jesus said to him, 'Do not forbid him, for he who is not against us is on our side.'"[88] So often our pride may blind us from understanding those in the 'other camp'. The attitude of some is that any difference from how they see it is harmful. Maybe we are missing the point though, that Jesus wants to build the Church, marriages, families, friendships, and the world with those who are communing with Him today.

Serving the World: Liturgy after the Liturgy

During a time when most people were almost exclusively concerned with their own survival, how inspiring it must have been for people to see Christians prepared to serve the world, to engage in 'liturgy after the Liturgy.' Liturgy does not conclude when the priest sends the congregation into the world with his invocation to, "Go in peace, the Peace of the Lord be with you all," but rather to summon liturgy to continue into the world. The Christian faithful are instructed to go out into the world and do their work of 'shining the light of Christ,' which they received in them.

Cyprian of Carthage describes how there was no difference in the death rates between Christians and non-Christians but there *was* a significant difference in the way each group lived their final days:

> The just are dying with the unjust, it is not for you to think that the destruction is a common one for both the evil and the good...How suitable, how necessary it is that this plague and pestilence, which seems horrible and deadly, searches out the justice of each and every one and

---

[88] Luke 9:49-50.

examines the minds of the human race; whether the well care for the sick, whether relatives dutifully love their kinsmen as they should, whether masters show compassion for their ailing slaves, whether physicians do not desert the afflicted.[89]

Cyprian describes a time when the Christian seemed to almost welcome the great epidemic of his time as a means to serve their communities. Dionysius of Alexandria, a contemporary of Cyprian, sees the plague merely as "schooling and testing"[90] through which the Christians could grow and offer service to those who rejected them, just as Jesus Christ had done to a world that crucified Him. During the ravaging of Alexandria by the Cyprian Plague, "peace was reinforced...during which the pagan population was distracted from harassing the Christians. In fact, the Christians rendered a positive service to their enemies by helping to bury their dead and by comforting the sick."[91] A further description is found in a Festal Letter to the brethren in Alexandria by Dionysius:

At all events most of the brethren through their love and brotherly affection for us spared not themselves nor abandoned one another, but without regard to their own peril visited those who fell sick, diligently looking after and ministering to them and cheerfully shared their fate with them, being infected with the disease from them and willingly involving themselves in their troubles. Not a few also, after nursing others back to recovery, died themselves, taking death over from them and thus fulfilling in very deed the common saying, which is taken always as a note of mere good feeling; for in their departure they became their expiatory substitutes. At all events, the very pick of our brethren lost their lives in this way, both priests and deacons and some highly praised ones from among the laity, so that this manner of dying

[89] Cyprian of Carthage, *On Mortality, 15.*

[90] Eusebius of Caesarea, *Church History, VII, 22.*

[91] Aziz S. Atiya, "Dionysius the Great," in *The Coptic Encyclopedia* (Claremont, 1991), 909a-912a.

does not seem far removed from martyrdom, being the outcome of much piety and stalwart faith. So, too, taking up the bodies of the saints on their arms and breasts, closing their eyes and shutting their mouths, bearing them on their shoulders and laying them out for burial, clinging to them, embracing them, washing them, decking them out, they not long after had the same services rendered to them; for many of the survivors followed in their train. But the Gentiles behaved quite differently: those who were beginning to fall sick they thrust away, and their dearest they fled from, or cast them half dead into the roads: unburied bodies they treated as vile refuse; for they tried to avoid the spreading and communication of the fatal disease, difficult as it was to escape for all their scheming.[92]

Through their love for their fellow Christians, which extended beyond the family of God to those who attacked them, the faithful were branded as disciples of Christ and were able to glorify God through the process.

In our COVID-19 crisis, we must find creative opportunities to extend such love to one another as well as to those who are *beyond the walls of the Church*, while at the same time honoring local laws and guidelines of health agencies. By our love for one another, the world will know that we are Christ's disciples. Whether it is in delivering groceries or medication for those who are immunocompromised, elderly, or sick, our service to another should not just be done before man, but as a love offering to God and unto one another. This love cannot be put under a lampstand but must be extended into the world. What a tremendous act of love it was when His Holiness Pope Tawadros II, following nationwide closures in Egypt, transformed some churches and monasteries into factories for

---

[92] Eusebius of Caesarea, *Church History, VII, 22.*

producing masks to be distributed to the general public.[93] What a great act of humility it is for many to willingly wear face masks in public, if for nothing else, to be protective of the physical and emotional health of their neighbors. How beautiful it is when Christians are producing verse cards and bracelets with encouraging messages to be distributed to both the healthcare workers and the infected in order to lift their spirits at times of great despair. What a wonderful labor of love it is for members of the church to prepare Easter meals and distribute them to community members who are unable to prepare their own meals. What a great reflection of God's love in the world to reach out to first responders – such as personnel at police departments, fire stations, and emergency medical services – to provide meals for them.[94] It is truly an incredible site to witness intentional, sacrificial acts of love emanating from the Body of Jesus Christ.

---

[93]Hazem Rifaat, "A Nun Operator that Begins Manufacturing Masks and Medical Uniforms," الفجر بوابة, April 4, 2020, https://www.elfagr.news/3911466.

[94] During the weeks following the COVID-19 Pandemic lockdown, the members of St. Anianus Coptic Orthodox Church engaged in various services, including the distribution of 250 bracelets to healthcare workers with encouraging messages, establishing a service to provide 'ear-savers' (to help protect against ear chafing from face masks) to healthcare workers who wear face masks over 9 hours a day, meals for 20% of Church families who could not provide for themselves due to illness or other circumstances, amongst other services. All members engaged in the various services, including both the children and the elderly, according to their abilities.

Conclusion

ometimes I wonder how easy it is to theorize a
conversation into formulas when a pandemic is sweeping a
world beyond yours. When you personally have been
touched by a plague that has engulfed your own world, it
transforms you. I believe it makes you more human. The world is at a
crossroads. Just as various plagues, famines, and eras of persecution
have transformed the world before us, I am hopeful that the Church
will be part of this transformation in our Coronavirus world.
Christians must not reduce the faith to doing that which has always
been comfortable for them. They must also avoid seeing their faith as
a means to seek some special 'protection or privilege from God.'
Rather than being obsessed with self-preservation of life, rituals, or
personal comfort, Christ is calling us to be consumed with fulfilling
our role in showing Christ's salvation and love to the entire world.
The unprecedented growth of the Church did not come because
Christians from past generations strategized or planned better than
others. History is clear that the Orthodox Church belongs to a
'tradition of diversity.' Her ability to be flexible in various times of
crisis allowed her to always reflect the image of God to the world and

to serve the needs of a suffering people. Although we may learn lessons from past generations, the circumstances and opportunities of today are unique. Rather than simply attempting to plagiarize a response from past generations, Christians today must be prepared to uphold our 'tradition of diversity' by seeking what is suitable for our context. It may be tempting to simply attempt to borrow from previous generations, as it may appear 'traditional and safe enough.' We do not find such a response from our Christians ancestors. Their faith was rarely – if ever – safe. They joyfully served those infected by disease, went to caves to baptize their children, communed in variety of ways, converted their homes into churches, utilized different substances for communion, became martyrs for Christ, and much more. They did not do this because others before them had done so. Every incident demanded a different response and the Church was not afraid to take drastic steps. With a proper theological paradigm and spiritual trajectory, they were able to discern the difference between essence and form, thus allowing them to engage with the challenges of the day for the purpose of sharing Christ's healing grace in the world.

These were people who truly walked by an enlightened faith. God is calling His people to turn to Him so that the land might be healed, as he says "if My people who are called by My name will humble themselves, and pray and seek My face, and turn from their wicked ways, then I will hear from heaven, and will forgive their sin and heal their land".[95] Let us return to God being compelled by His unchanging love, reflecting the sacrificial-life of the risen Christ, and enlightened by the Holy Spirit, in order to authentically reflect the life of the Holy Trinity in our new reality of a Coronavirus world.

---

[95] 2 Chronicles 7:14.

Appendix

Coptic Orthodox Patriarchate

طريكة الأنبا طالأرثوذكس

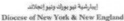

إيبارشية نيو يورك ونيو إنجلاند
Diocese of New York & New England

المقر البابوي بأمريكا الشمالية
Archdiocese of North America

Saturday, March 14, 2020

Joint Statement Concerning Coronavirus Disease 2019 (COVID-19)

During these trying times of pandemic, we are certain of and grateful for God's constant protection of the Church and the entire world. As we work together to overcome these challenges and care for those in need, we remain faithful in our Almighty God, His abiding love and care for His children, and His presence within the Church, the Ark of Salvation. We trust that this trial shall pass soon and God's promise that "He shall deliver you from the snare of the fowler and from the perilous pestilence" (Psalm 91:3) shall be fulfilled.

In view of the current Coronavirus disease (COVID-19) outbreak, and in keeping with our responsibility as Christians to care for our brothers and sisters throughout the world, we are closely following the guidance and recommendations of the Centers for Disease Control (CDC) and other public health authorities. Accordingly, the Coptic Orthodox Archdiocese of North America and the Coptic Orthodox Diocese of New York and New England have implemented the following protocol in an abundance of caution, with the safety of our congregations and our broader communities in mind, and with an aim to mitigate the spread of COVID-19.

1. **Liturgical:** Although all non-liturgical services have been immediately suspended in all of our churches until further notice, we are especially blessed and thankful to be able to receive the Life-Giving Mystery of the Holy Body and the Precious Blood of our Lord Jesus Christ for the healing of our souls, bodies and spirits as being "the medicine of immortality" and the cornerstone of our Coptic Orthodox Church since her inception by our Lord, Jesus Christ. During this time, the faithful are encouraged to use caution when attending Liturgy and are urged to use prudence through appropriate social distancing. For example, when greeting one another, you are asked to greet without touching (as during Pascha Week). If the elderly will attend liturgy during this time, they are encouraged to do so during weekdays, when attendance is expected to be lighter. The faithful are requested to bring their own personal head coverings, personal corporals, and water bottles

2. **Limited Services:** In lieu of suspended in-person meetings, agape meals, spiritual days, retreats, etc., each church shall implement interactive on-line tools to provide teaching and spiritual fellowship

3. **Hygiene:** For the most up-to-date information on hygiene, please visit the CDC website at https://www.cdc.gov/coronavirus/2019-ncov/prepare/prevention.html. As part of these precautions, please note that members are required to stay home and seek medical attention if they are sick with any symptoms (e.g. fever, pressure in the chest, shortness of breath, or coughing, etc.). Additionally, please exercise good hygiene, which includes

- 1 -

coughing and sneezing into your elbow or a tissue. Avoid touching eyes, nose or mouth, as viruses can transfer from hands to bodies. Wash hands frequently with water and soap, and especially after coughing, sneezing or using tissues

We will stay in close communication over the coming weeks regarding updates and any changes in plan. Please continue to communicate with your local priest regarding any questions or concerns.

As you may know, Sunday, March 15th has been declared a National Day of Prayer for the current circumstances. Let us all unite in constant prayer for the recovery of the world, our nation, and all the sick, especially those who are infected with COVID-19. We ask for the protection of our Lord upon all humanity and that each person responds with a repentant heart.

CHURCH LIFE IN A CORONAVIRUS WORLD

Coptic Orthodox Patriarchate بطريركية الأقباط الأرثوذكس

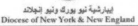
إيبارشية نيو يورك ونيو إنجلاند
Diocese of New York & New England

المقر البابوي بأمريكا الشمالية
Archdiocese of North America

Monday, March 16, 2020

2nd Joint Statement Concerning Coronavirus Disease (COVID-19)

Due to the rapidly evolving situation surrounding the Coronavirus pandemic ("COVID-19"), the Coptic Orthodox Church must comply with the guidelines of the Centers for Disease Control ("CDC") and other public health authorities to limit gatherings to very small numbers. Effective immediately, the churches of the Coptic Orthodox Archdiocese in New Jersey and the Diocese of New York and New England **will limit liturgical attendance strictly to priests and select deacons.** Moreover, it is mandated that any church from which a congregant has tested positive for COVID-19 must close for a minimum of two (2) weeks. These measures are being taken as part of the Church's efforts to mitigate the spread of the virus and safeguard the health and well-being of the faithful. Currently, several members of the Coptic community have tested positive for COVID-19.

Our faith in the holy Body and the precious Blood of our Lord is beyond doubt. We know that partaking of the holy, life-giving and healing mysteries, in the words of St. Ignatius, is "the medicine of immortality and the antidote to sin." At the same time, the Church must legally, morally, and spiritually act responsibly by actively participating in social distancing and following guidelines of the CDC and local health authorities.

His Grace Bishop David and the fathers of the churches are committed to continue praying liturgies and offering the oblations during these trying times on behalf of their respective congregations, while it is still legally permissible and in accordance with guidelines. We ask that our congregations participate in the liturgy by live streaming, as well as participate in Sunday school, Bible study, youth group virtual meetings, and additional services, all of which will be made available online. Additionally, each parish shall provide its congregation with a call-in number which may be used for guidance and support for our parishioners.

We are united in prayer with our brothers and sisters in Egypt and throughout the world, under the leadership and guidance of our holy father His Holiness Pope Tawadros II, who sent us the following message: **"The Lord Jesus Christ protect you all. It is an exceptional period which shall pass speedily and normal life shall be resumed. My sincere love and wishes for recovery, health and peace."**

May our Lord provide healing for all of humanity and strengthen your faith through His presence.

- 1 -

The Motherhood of the Church[96]

The Church over generations has always been a "mother" who cares for the well-being of Her children, paying attention to the physical, spiritual, and emotional aspects of their lives. Her seven sacraments are the foundation of Her faith and godliness over the years as witnessed by Her history.

The enemy of goodness is the one who, from time to time, instigates doubts in this orthodox faith by rumors, heresies, lies, and falsehoods. The Church, through Her fathers and congregation, has always stood in defense against any deviation of faith and doctrine, as She not only knows the faith, but lives this faith daily.

The Church, being guided by the Holy Spirit, has to face the circumstances that change from time to time, and as some fathers said "The Church makes the Eucharist and the Eucharist makes the Church." What is important is to offer the sacrament, whether in homes, caves, catacombs, fields, or churches. What is important is the sacrament.

The holy Body and Blood of Christ, i.e. the real non-metaphorical presence of Christ, do not transmit any disease as they are the Mystery of life, and far be it for anyone to say otherwise.

The methods of distributing the Sacrament have changed in form over the years, but the goal of offering the Sacrament of Holy Communion has always been the same, despite changes in the means and methods that are being used.

---

[96] HH Pope Tawadros II, "Motherhood of the Church." *Facebook*, 27 June 2020, 3:04 pm EET, https://www.facebook.com/554483354589807/posts/3161539443884172/. Accessed 27 June 2020.

Christ's call has been to "Come to Me, all you who labor and are heavy laden, and I will give you rest" (Matthew 11:28). He also said "I desire mercy and not sacrifice" (Matthew 12:7). Not all the Christian believers are strong in faith, but the duty of the Church is to shepherd, help and serve them. The Church does not only serve those who are strong in faith, but also those who have weak faith, those of little faith, and those of limited faith, as well as sinners of every kind. Christ did not come to call the righteous, but sinners to repentance, and He said "Those who are well [strong] have no need of a physician, but those who are sick" (Mark 2:17).

The Church listens to the call of the person who is crying out "help my unbelief" and She has to respond under the current circumstances.

Two methods of distributing the Mystery of Holy Communion have been settled upon in the Coptic Orthodox Church, and they are:

The first method: The conventional, customary, and well-known method in all of our churches where the prayers and rites of the Divine Liturgy are celebrated with the consecrated altar utensils.

The second method: The alternative method that is being used to administer Communion to those who are sick at homes or hospitals, and to the prisoners in prisons. This method may be used in church as an exception when there are large numbers of communicants with only one priest present. There are many documented references for this in the holy Euchologion book, and it is neither a heresy, nor a deviation, nor a degradation to the sanctity of the Mystery.

On the same scale, we, in practicing the Mystery, use stone altars consecrated with the Holy Myron Oil. We can also use any wooden or non-wooden table with a Holy Tablet that is consecrated with the Holy Myron Oil placed on it, as an exception until there is a permanent and consecrated altar. This does not belittle the Sacrament of Holy Communion at all.

At the time of the institution of the Mystery, there was no global pandemic that killed hundreds of thousands of people, and infected millions in most countries of the world. This is a time of disease and infection. This is a time that needs prevention and extreme caution.

In the temptation of the Lord Christ, the Devil said to Him, "If You are the Son of God, throw Yourself down from here." While the Lord Christ could have done that, but He answered and said to him, "You shall not tempt the Lord your God" (Luke 4:12).

God is not ungrateful, cruel, or dulled. Far be it!

God is merciful, compassionate, and laments human condition and weakness. It is written: "Therefore be merciful, just as your Father also is merciful" (Luke 6:36).

+ This is a time of repentance and not a time of speeches or articles ... "but unless you repent you will all likewise perish" (Luke 13:5).

+ This is a time of regret and preparation, and not a time of stubbornness and cruelty ... "Rise and pray, lest you enter into temptation" (Luke 22:46).

+ This is a time for tears, and not a time for showing off and debate ... "Lord, save me!" (Matthew 14:30).

"For what profit is it to a man if he gains the whole world, and is himself destroyed or lost?" (Luke 9:25). What would be the benefit for anyone who writes and posts on social media and attacks the Church and Her fathers, and Her plans causing the people to be upset and to suffer? Most likely, repentance did not find its way to you. To you I say: Watch out! Death is at the door; "this night your soul will be required of you" and your eternal life is more important than anything (Luke 12:20).

In the Holy Bible, we see Saint Paul the Apostle becoming weak to win the souls of the weak. Consequently, the Church, as a mother, is applying the rules of love during this time of crisis of the pandemic's global spread, and uses the method of giving Communion to the sick -as an exception- which is a method mentioned in the rituals according to the Euchologion of Fr. Abd al-Masih al-Masoudi al-Baramousi (1902) instead of the usual method, to which we will revert once normal conditions return. This is a suspension or a deferral of the usual way, not a cancellation or an omission. This is the voice of wisdom, especially since we do not live alone in this society. We must not be a cause of confusion for anyone or a stumble to the souls we love.

The call for preventive action as a result of the recent circumstances is not a deviation from the faith at all. We are seeing hundreds of deaths, thousands of infected, and a severe outbreak; The pandemic has exceeded the capacities of hospitals, doctors, and equipment.

There is nothing else for us to do other than to seek mercy from God that He may have compassion on all of us, on our country, on our Church and on our children.

(Signed)
H.H. Pope Tawadros II

Bibliography

"2nd Joint Statement Concerning Coronavirus Disease (COVID-19)." Coptic Orthodox Archdiocese of North America and Coptic Orthodox Diocese of New York & New England, March 16, 2020.

Adel, Rafik, and Fr. Misael Al-Baramousi. "Preserving the Eucharistic Bread and the Rite of Reconstructing the Chalice." *Alexandria School Journal*, no. 21 (February 2016): 123–45.

Alexandria, Athanasius of. *On the Incarnation*. Translated by John Behr. Yonkers, NY: St. Vladimir's Seminary Press, 2011.

Antioch, Ignatius of. *Epistle to Philadelphia*, n.d.

Atiya, Aziz S. "Dionysius the Great." In *The Coptic Encyclopedia*, 909a–12. Claremont, 1991.

Bray, R. S. *Armies of Pestilence: The Impact of Disease on History*. James Clarke & Co., 2004.

Byrne, Joseph Patrick. *Encyclopedia of the Black Death*. ABC-CLIO, 2012.

Caesarea, Eusebius of. *Church History*. Vol. 7, n.d.

Carthage, Cyprian of. *On Mortality*, n.d.

CDC. "Coronavirus Disease 2019 (COVID-19) - Get Your Community- and Faith-Based Organizations Ready for Coronavirus Disease 2019." Centers for Disease Control and Prevention, February 11, 2020. https://www.cdc.gov/coronavirus/2019-ncov/community/organizations/guidance-community-faith-organizations.html.

Coptic Synaxarium. Vol. 2, n.d.

"COVID-19 Joint Statement." Coptic Orthodox Archdiocese of North America and Coptic Orthodox Diocese of New York & New England, March 14, 2020.

Dahir, Abdi Latif. "'Instead of Coronavirus, the Hunger Will Kill Us.' A Global Food Crisis Looms. - The New York Times," April 22, 2020.

https://www.nytimes.com/2020/04/22/world/africa/coronavir
us-hunger-crisis.html.

Delkeskamp-Hayes, Corinna. "Why Patients Should Give Thanks
for Their Disease: Traditional Christianity on the Joy of
Suffering." *Christian Bioethics* 12, no. 2 (August 1, 2006):
213–28. https://doi.org/10.1080/13803600600805609.

Hippo, Augustine of. *City of God.* Vol. 10,6, n.d.

"History of the Patriarchs: Deir Al-Syrian Edition," n.d.

Irenaeus of Lyons. *Against the Heresies.* Vol. 4, 180AD.

Jerusalem, Cyril of. *Catechetical Lectures.* Vol. XXI, 350AD.

Labib, Subhi, and Aziz S. Atiya. "Cosmas." In *The Coptic
Encyclopedia*, 636b–37. Claremont, 1991.

———. "Isaac." In *The Coptic Encyclopedia*, 13031–1303b.
Claremont, 1991.

Lane, Edward William. *An Account of the Manners and Customs of
the Modern Egyptians.* John Murray, 1860.

Liturgy in a Time of Plague. "Liturgy in a Time of Plague: A Letter
to a Colleague." Accessed May 8, 2020.
http://abmcg.blogspot.com/2020/03/liturgy-in-time-of-
plague.html.

Martyr, Justin. *Apology.* Vol. 1, n.d.

"Modern Lab Reaches across the Ages to Resolve Plague DNA
Debate." Accessed May 8, 2020.
https://phys.org/news/2013-05-modern-lab-ages-plague-
dna.html.

Nyssa, Gregory of. *The Great Catechism*, n.d.

Ousterhout, Robert. "Rebuilding the Temple: Constantine
Monomachus and the Holy Sepulchre." *The Journal of the
Society of Architectural Historians* 48, no. 1 (March 1989):
66–78.

Ancient History Encyclopedia. "Reactions to Plague in the Ancient
& Medieval World." Accessed May 14, 2020.
https://www.ancient.eu/article/1534/reactions-to-plague-in-
the-ancient--medieval-world/.

Release, Press. "The Church without the Eucharist Is Not the
Church - Interview with John Zizioulas." *Anglican Ink* ©

2020 (blog), April 1, 2020. http://anglican.ink/2020/03/31/the-church-without-the-eucharist-is-not-the-church-interview-with-john-zizioulas/.

Review, Princeton. *Cracking the AP World History Exam, 2018 Edition.* Random House Children's Books, 2017.

Rifaat, Hazem. "A Nun Operator That Begins Manufacturing Maskss and Medical Uniforms." الفجر بوابة, April 4, 2020. https://www.elfagr.news/3911466.

Severus of Al'Ashmunein (Hermopolis). *History of the Patriarchs of the Coptic Church of Alexandria: Part 4: Mennas I - Joseph (849 AD).* Vol. 10. Patrologia Orientalis, 1910.

———. *History of the Patriarchs of the Coptic Church of Alexandria: Peter I - Benjamin I (661 AD). Pp. 383-518 (Pp.119-256 of Text).* Vol. 2. Patrologia Orientalis, 1904.

European Centre for Disease Prevention and Control. "Situation Update Worldwide, as of 24 April 2020." Epidemiological Updates, April 24, 2020. https://www.ecdc.europa.eu/en/geographical-distribution-2019-ncov-cases.

Spanel, Donald, and Tim Vivian. "Peter I." In *The Coptic Encyclopedia*, edited by Aziz S. Atiya, 1943a–47. Claremont, 1991.

Stark, Rodney. *The Triumph of Christianity: How the Jesus Movement Became the World's Largest Religion.* New York: Harper One, 2011.

Taft, Robert. "Byzantine Communion Rites: The Early Ritual of Clergy Communion." *OCP*, no. 65 (1999): 307–45.

The Apostolic Constitution. Vol. VIII, 380AD.

The Druze in the Middle East: Their Faith, Leadership, Identity and Status. Brighton England ; Portland, Or: Sussex Academic Press, 2003.

"The Epidemiological Characteristics of an Outbreak of 2019 Novel Coronavirus Diseases (COVID-19)." *China CDC Weekly* 2, no. 8 (2020): 113–22.

Toner, Jerry. *Roman Disasters.* John Wiley & Sons, 2018.

Woolley, Reginald Maxwell. *The Bread of the Eucharist.* London,

UK: A.R. Mowbray & Co. Ltd., 1913.

Yurochko, Brian David. "Cultural and Intellectual Responses to the Black Death." Electronic Theses and Dissertations, Duquesne University, 2009.

ABOUT THE AUTHOR

Rev. Fr. Michael Sorial is a parish priest at St. Anianus Coptic Orthodox Church in Monroe Township, New Jersey. He is Co-founder and President of Agora University. He holds a Master of Letters degree in Divinity from St. Mary's College, University of St. Andrews, Scotland. Fr. Michael's thesis focused on the Patristic Ecclesiology of the Indigenous Orthodox Churches in North America. He is currently working on his Doctorate of Ministry at Pittsburgh Theological Seminary in Pennsylvania, USA. Fr. Michael is a husband and father of three, as well as a missionary, author and lecturer on various topics including Orthodox Mission, Youth development, Catechism, Church History, Contemporary Orthodox living, and Ecclesiology.

Other Titles by the Author:

- *Incarnational Exodus: A Vision for the Coptic Orthodox Church in North America Based on the Incarnational Theology of Athanasius of Alexandria*

Thank you for reading! Please add a short review on Amazon to share your thoughts with the author!

AGORA
UNIVERSITY
PRESS

Made in the USA
Middletown, DE
25 July 2020

13671294R00045